Sight Words

Level B

55 More Words
you need to know
to be a successful reader

Written by Shannon Keeley • Illustrated by Christy Schneider

FlashKids

Spark Publishing
120 Fifth Avenue
New York, NY 10011

ISBN-13: 978-1-4114-0492-2
ISBN-10: 1-4114-0492-0

For more information, please visit *www.flashkidsbooks.com*
Please submit changes or report errors to *www.flashkidsbooks.com/errors*

Printed and bound in China

Dear Parent,

Every time your child reads a text, 50–75% of the words he or she encounters are from the Dolch Sight Word List. The Dolch Sight Word List is a core group of 220 common words that are repeated frequently in reading material. Children need extra practice learning these words, many of which can't be represented by simple pictures. Often, these sight words do not follow regular spelling rules and cannot be "sounded out." So, learning to immediately recognize these words "at sight" is a critical skill for fluent reading. This is the second book in a series that covers all 220 Dolch sight words. The 55 words covered in this book are listed below. The activities in this book offer lots of practice with tracing and writing, as well as fun word puzzles and games. Your child can color the pictures, laugh at the funny characters, and enjoy learning about sight words.

The sight words included in this book are:

after	could	her	please	they
again	do	him	pretty	this
any	eat	how	ride	too
are	every	into	round	under
as	four	let	saw	want
at	from	must	say	well
ate	get	new	she	went
black	give	now	some	white
brown	going	of	soon	who
by	had	our	thank	will
came	have	out	there	with

came

Say the word **came** aloud as you trace it.

came

Now practice writing the word once on each line.

I _____ home late.

Stay on Track

Find the word **came** on each track and circle it.

c a m c a m e c m e

m c a m e c a e m e

a m e c a m c a m e

Circle all the words that spell **came**.

came

caim

came

came

cam

came

kame

cane

came

 **black**

say the word black aloud as you trace it.

Now practice writing the word once on each line.

I saw a _____ bear.

Maze Craze

Help the bee find its way through the maze.
Connect the letters b-l-a-c-k to make the word
black.

four

say the word four aloud as you trace it.

four

Now practice writing the word once on each line.

I am _____ years old.

Out of Order

The letters for the word **four** are out of order! If the letters can be unscrambled to make the word **four**, write the word on the line. If not, leave it blank.

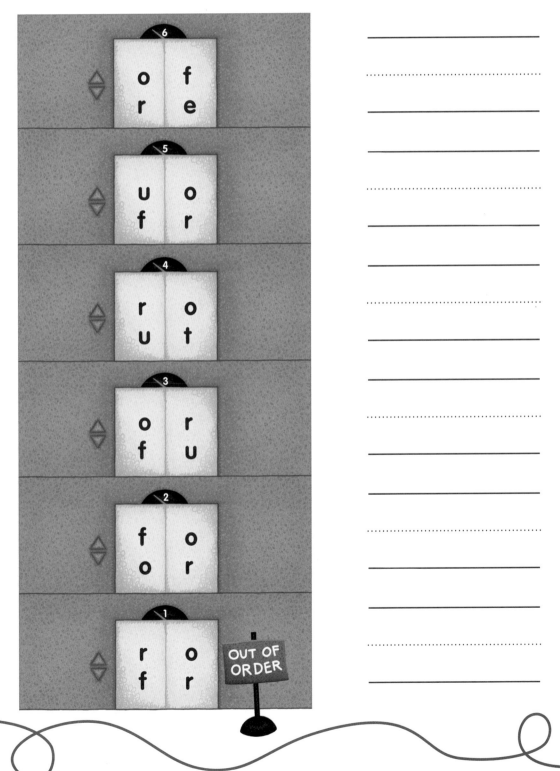

_____

. . . .

_____

. . . .

_____

. . . .

_____

. . . .

_____

. . . .

_____

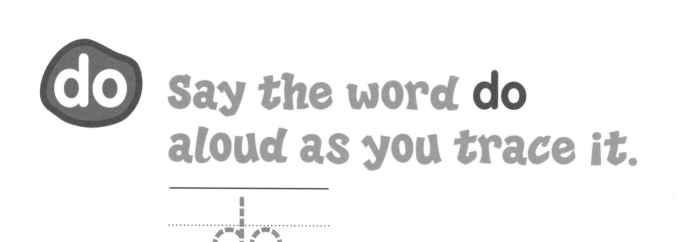

do **say the word do aloud as you trace it.**

do

Now practice writing the word once on each line.

What _____ you want to eat?

Three Cheers

Circle the word **do** every time it appears. Count the number of circled words in each cheer and write it in the box.

Do we want to win?
Yes, we do!
We'll do all we can.
How about you?

We'll do just great!
We'll do our best.
How do we do it?
We'll do better than
the rest!

Team A

Team B

Which team's cheer has the higher number? _____

 Say the word too aloud as you trace it.

.·:ẗöö

Now practice writing the word once on each line.

It's _____ hot.

Hide and Seek

Some of the words in the treetop have too hidden inside. Find the words and write them on the lines below. Circle the letters t-o-o in each word.

stop   tool   toe
                              tooth
town   toot
        cartoon   toad
    stoop
                stool

too

_____

_____

_____

_____

_____

Review: Word Search

Find each word in the word search.

| came | black | four | do | too |

```
b  t  o  o  f
l  l  c  m  o
a  o  a  k  u
c  f  m  c  r
d  o  e  d  k
```

Color the row that has all five review words spelled correctly.

1.	2.	3.	4.	5.
back	tou	came	bak	four
due	four	do	came	too
came	do	four	do	cawe
foar	came	too	too	do
too	back	black	four	back

Review: Black Out!

Read each sentence, then find the missing word in the boxes. Put an X through all the boxes that show the missing word.

A.

black	too
do	four

B.

came	do
black	too

1. It was _____ muddy to play outside.

2. So we _____ inside.

3. Later, Mom saw _____ mud on the floor.

4. I didn't _____ it!

5. My dog had left _____ muddy footprints.

Which square has all its boxes marked off first? _____

Say the word into aloud as you trace it.

into

Now practice writing the word once on each line.

I fell _____ the hole.

Crack the Code

The word **into** is hidden once in each line. Find the word and circle the letters. Then use the code to complete the riddle below.

i	n	t	o	n	t	o	t
#	=	<	@	X	+	*	&

i	n	t	n	i	n	t	o
<	@	#	=	*	X	+	&

Why is the moon always so tired?

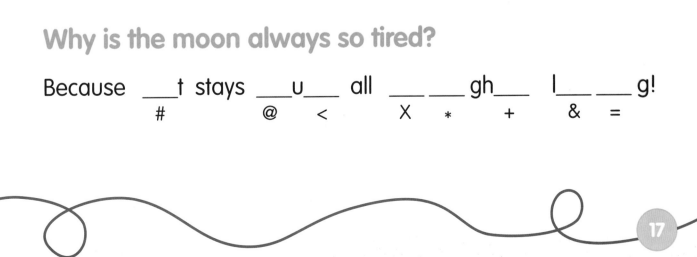

Because ___t stays ___u___ all ___ ___ gh___ l___ ___ g!
      #   @   <   X   *   +   &   =

 **are** **Say the word are aloud as you trace it.**

_____

are

Now practice writing the word once on each line.

We _____ dancers.

Tic-Tac-Toe

Circle the row that spells the word **are**.

a	e	r
e	r	e
a	e	e

Circle the row that has the word **are** three times.

are	are	aer
art	are	are
are	are	arr

going say the word going aloud as you trace it.

Now practice writing the word once on each line.

I am _____ to school.

The Finish Line

Draw a line to the flag with the letters that finish the word **going**.

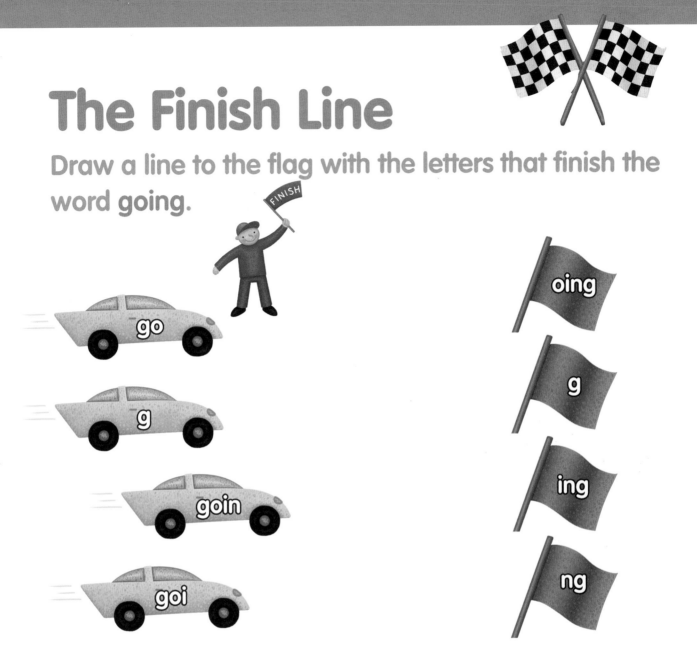

Do the letters in the flags make the word **going**?
Circle Yes or No.

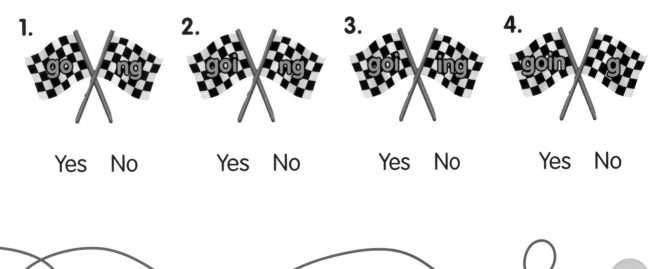

1. Yes   No

2. Yes   No

3. Yes   No

4. Yes   No

have

Say the word have aloud as you trace it.

have

Now practice writing the word once on each line.

I _____ a new doll.

Word Hunt

The word **have** is in the story five times. Hunt for the word and circle it each time it appears.

Have you seen my hat? I have been looking for half the day. I need some help to find it. I usually hang it in the hall. I have a special hook for my hat. But it's not there!

I have to find it soon. My head needs a hat. It's the only hat I have!

Circle the hats with the word have inside.

1. have
2. hvae
3. have
4. have
5. hava
6. haev

at

say the word at aloud as you trace it.

at

Now practice writing the word once on each line.

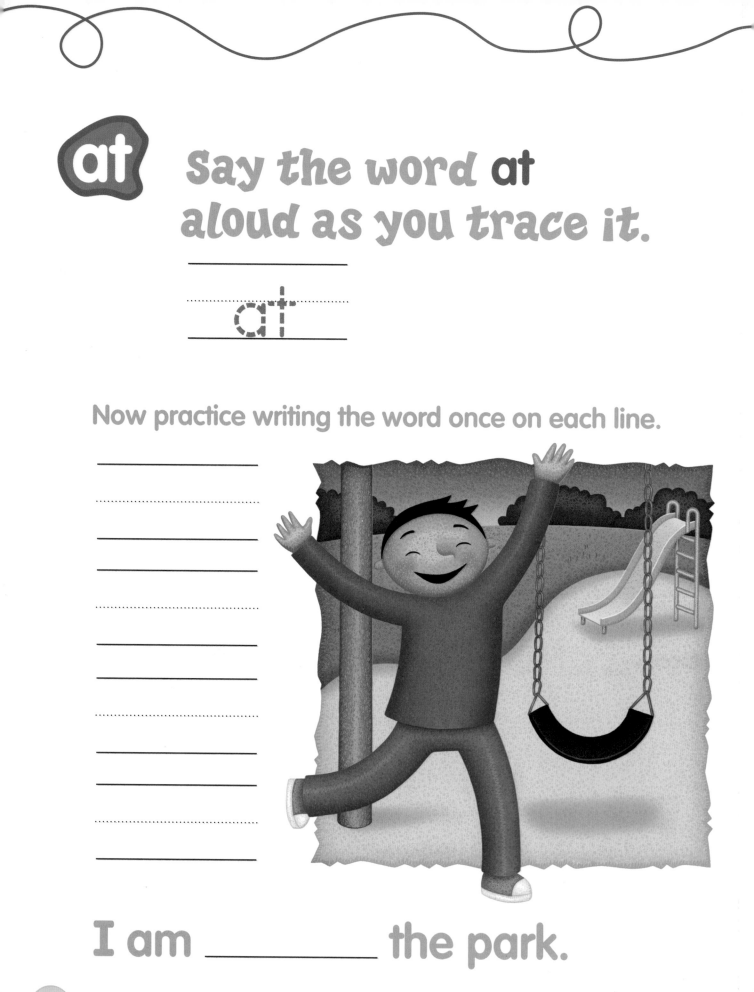

I am _____ the park.

Rhyme Time

Circle the pictures that rhyme with **at**. Underline the letters **a-t** in each word.

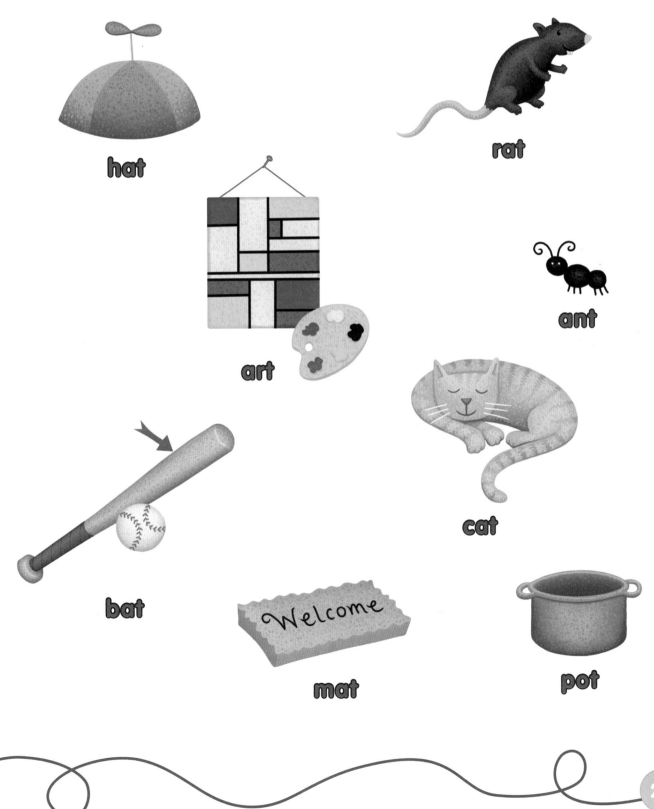

hat

rat

art

ant

bat

cat

mat

pot

Review: Word Search

Find each word in the word search.

into   are   going   have   at

```
h   a   v   e   i
a   v   n   i   o
g   o   i   n   g
a   r   e   t   o
t   g   h   o   n
```

Color the row that has all five review words spelled correctly.

1.	2.	3.	4.	5.
gonig	are	into	have	at
have	at	are	intoo	hane
are	imto	going	going	going
into	going	have	at	ane
att	hawe	at	are	into

Review: Story Code

Look for the review words as you read the story. Follow the code each time you see a review word.

(into) circle it

[going] make a box

✓at put a check

<u>are</u> underline

<u>have</u> wavy line

I always have my birthday party at home. This year, I wanted to have it someplace new.

"We are going somewhere different," my family said. "You are going to have a great time."

We all got into the car.

"Where are we going?" I asked.

"It's a surprise," they said. "You have to close your eyes."

"Are we there yet?" I asked.

"You have to be patient!" they said.

After a long drive, the car stopped.

"We're at the beach!" I said.

We all jumped into the water.

must say the word **must** aloud as you trace it.

must

Now practice writing the word once on each line.

You _____ go to bed.

Stay on Track

Find the word **must** on each track and circle it.

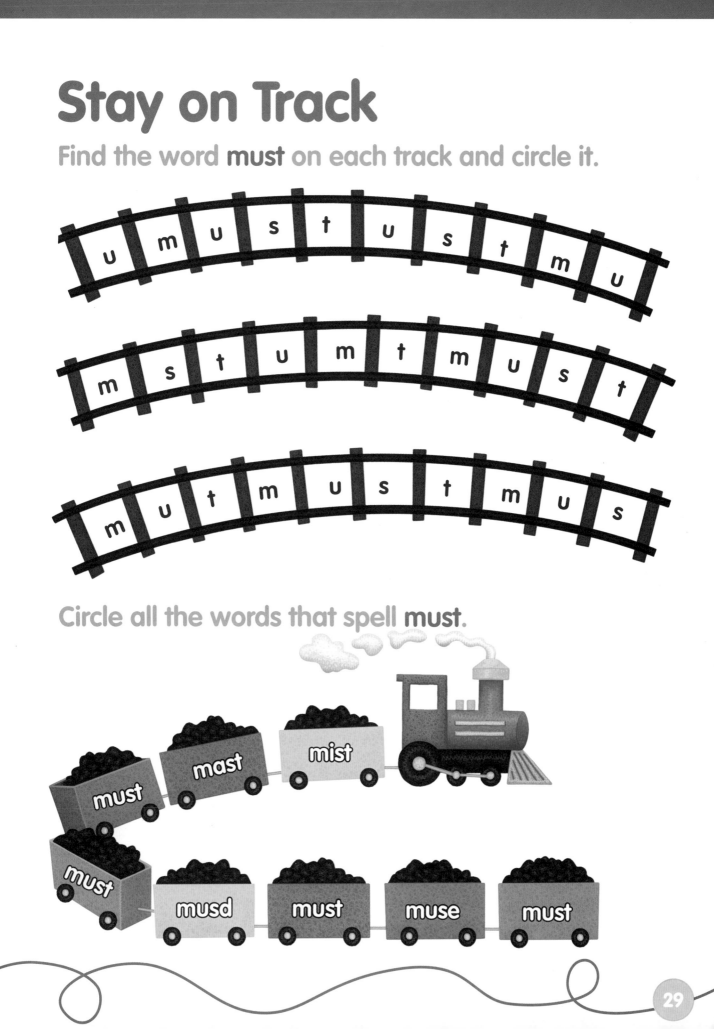

| u | m | u | s | t | u | s | t | m | u |

| m | s | t | u | m | t | m | u | s | t |

| m | u | t | m | u | s | t | m | u | s |

Circle all the words that spell **must**.

must   mast   mist

must

musd   must   muse   must

brown say the word brown aloud as you trace it.

brown

Now practice writing the word once on each line.

The peanuts are _____.

Maze Craze

Help the monkey find its way through the maze. Connect the letters **b-r-o-w-n** to make the word **brown**.

d

b

x

o

b

r

i

h

w

e

p

n

soon

say the word **soon** aloud as you trace it.

‾‾‾‾‾‾‾‾‾‾‾‾‾‾‾‾

soon

Now practice writing the word once on each line.

The pie will be done _____.

Out of Order

The letters for the word **soon** are out of order! If the letters can be unscrambled to make the word **soon**, write the word on the line. If not, leave it blank.

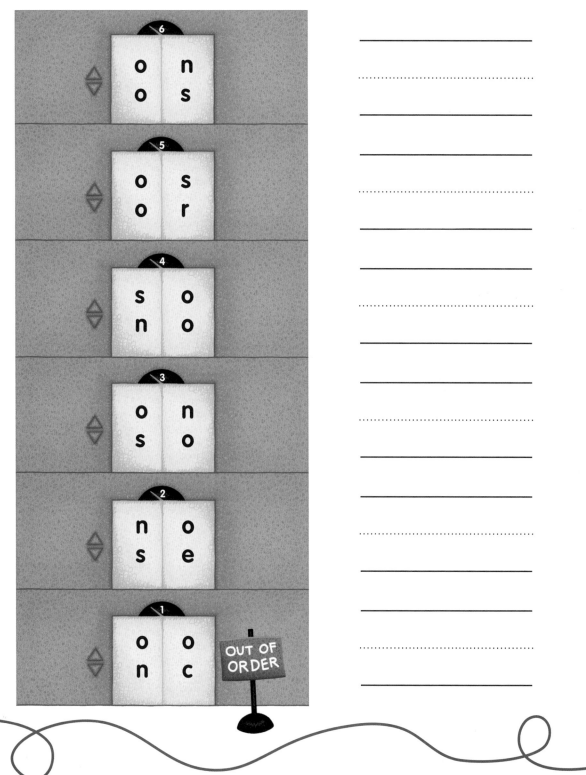

 **Say the word say aloud as you trace it.**

_____

say

Now practice writing the word once on each line.

You _____ it first.

Three Cheers

Circle the word **say** every time it appears. Count the number of circled words in each cheer and write it in the box.

When I say "go" you say "fight." Go! Go! Fight! Fight! When I say "win" you say "tonight." Win! Win! Tonight! Tonight!

You say you're so great. You say you're the best. But we're here to say we're better than the rest.

Team A

Team B

Which team's cheer has the higher number? _____

under

say the word under **aloud as** you trace it.

$\underline{\text{under}}$

Now practice writing the word once on each line.

My shoes are _____ the bed.

Hide and Seek

Some of the words in the treetop have **under** hidden inside. Find the words and write them on the lines below. Circle the letters **u-n-d-e-r** in each word.

blender thunder kinder underneath

wander wonderful

underground underwear

understand

under

_____

_____

_____

_____

_____

Review: Word Search

Find each word in the word search.

must   brown   soon   so   under

```
m  u  s     c  o
u  n  o  u  m
s  d  o  n  u
t  e  n  d  s
b  r  o  w  n
```

Color the row that has all five review words spelled correctly.

1.	2.	3.	4.	5.
ander	soon	broun	must	under
must	muzt	under	brown	so
soo	brown	must	soon	must
brown	under	soon	so	browm
soon	so	so	under	soom

Review: Black Out!

Read each sentence, then find the missing word in the boxes. Put an X through all the boxes that show the missing word.

A.

so	must
brown	under

B.

brown	soon
so	must

1. It's getting _____ late.

2. It will be time for bed _____.

3. First you _____ brush your teeth.

4. Don't forget your _____ teddy bear.

5. Get _____ the covers and fall asleep.

Which square has all its boxes marked off first? _____

Say the word ride aloud as you trace it.

ride

Now practice writing the word once on each line.

I can _____ my bike.

Crack the Code

The word ride is hidden once in each line. Find the word and circle the letters. Then use the code to complete the riddle below.

d	r	i	d	e	r	i	d
*	#	+	@	X	<	=	&

i	r	d	r	i	d	e	r
X	@	X	=	*	<	&	+

Why did the girl put her umbrella in her piggy bank?

She want___ ___ to sav___ ___t fo___ a ___a___ny
         X   @   &   *   =   #   +

___ay.
<

 **say the word get aloud as you trace it.**

get

Now practice writing the word once on each line.

Can I _____ a candy bar?

Tic-Tac-Toe

Circle the row that spells the word **get**.

e	t	g
g	e	t
g	t	e

Circle the row that has the word **get** three times.

got	pet	get
get	get	gte
get	get	gel

 **say the word after aloud as you trace it.**

Now practice writing the word once on each line.

You can have dessert _____ dinner.

The Finish Line

Draw a line to the flag with the letters that finish the word **after**.

Do the letters in the flags make the word **after**?
Circle Yes or No.

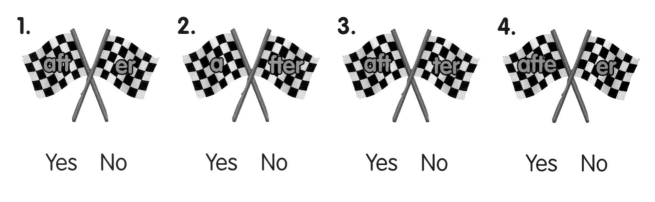

1.   Yes   No

2.   Yes   No

3.   Yes   No

4.   Yes   No

they

Say the word **they** aloud as you trace it.

they

Now practice writing the word once on each line.

_____ are my parents.

Word Hunt

The word **they** is in the story five times. Hunt for the word and circle it each time it appears.

I have twin brothers, Tim and Jim. They look exactly the same. They have brown hair and blue eyes. Today they have on matching clothes. Both of them are wearing white shirts and jeans. Hey, I can't tell them apart! I hope they tell me who is who. If not, then they will be in big trouble!

Circle the shirts with the word **they** inside.

1. thay
2. they
3. they
4. they
5. thy
6. then

 **say the word ate aloud as you trace it.**

ate

Now practice writing the word once on each line.

I _____ all the cake.

Rhyme Time

Circle the pictures that rhyme with **ate**. Underline the letters **a-t-e** in each word.

eat

date

bath

gate

boat

late

tape

plate

Review: Word Search

Find each word in the word search.

ride   get   after   they   ate

```
t  a  f  e  r
h  t  h  e  i
e  a  t  g  d
y  f  e  e  e
a  t  e  t  r
```

Color the row that has all five review words spelled correctly.

1.	2.	3.	4.	5.
gat	after	they	ate	ride
after	thye	ate	ride	get
atte	get	ribe	after	they
they	ride	get	gete	after
ride	ate	after	they	ate

Review: Story Code

Look for the review words as you read the story. Follow the code each time you see a review word.

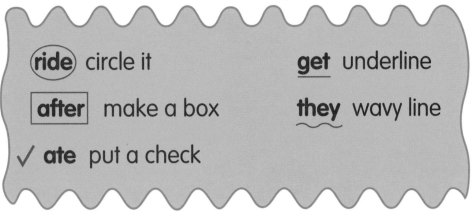

ride circle it

after make a box

✓ **ate** put a check

get underline

they wavy line

Amy and Ella went to the fair. First they saw the animals. A pony ate a carrot out of Ella's hand. After that, Ella wanted to go on a ride.

"Let's ride the Ferris wheel," Ella said.

"We need to get some tickets first," Amy said.

After they got tickets, they went on the ride. Then they decided to get hot dogs.

After they ate, they went home. They decided to come to the fair every year!

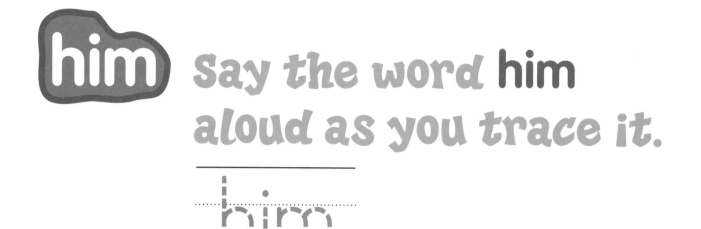 **say the word him aloud as you trace it.**

him

Now practice writing the word once on each line.

I sit next to _____.

Stay on Track

Find the word **him** on each track and circle it.

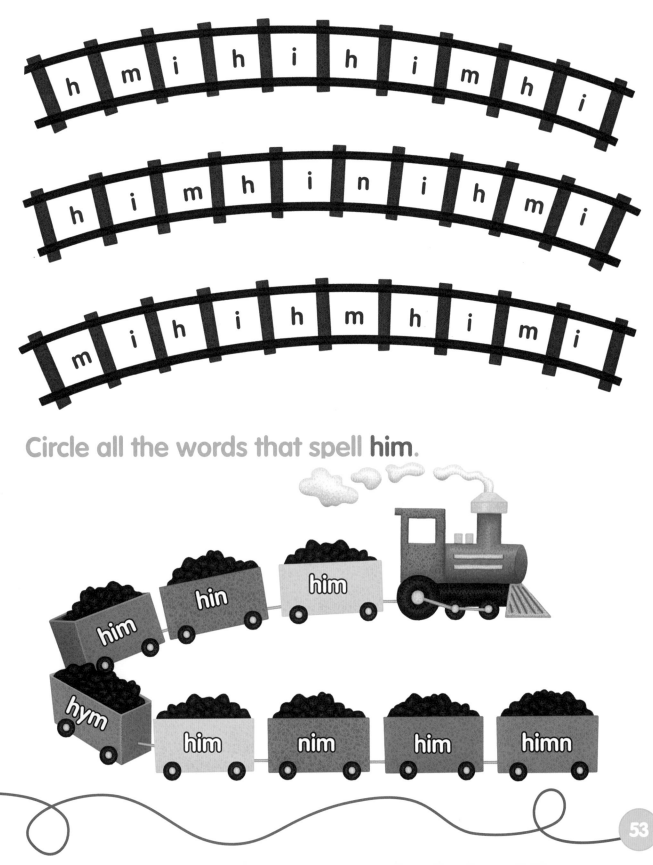

h | m | i | h | i | h | i | m | h | i

h | i | m | h | i | n | i | h | m | i

m | i | h | i | h | m | h | i | m | i

Circle all the words that spell **him**.

him

hin

him

hym

him

nim

him

himn

 **say the word please aloud as you trace it.**

please

Now practice writing the word once on each line.

May I _____ have some more?

Maze Craze

Help the fish find its way through the maze.
Connect the letters p-l-e-a-s-e to make the word
please.

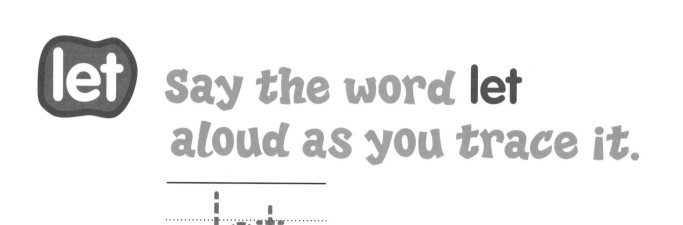

let say the word **let** aloud as you trace it.

let

Now practice writing the word once on each line.

Please _____ me in.

Out of Order

The letters for the word **let** are out of order! If the letters can be unscrambled to make the word **let**, write the word on the line. If not, leave it blank.

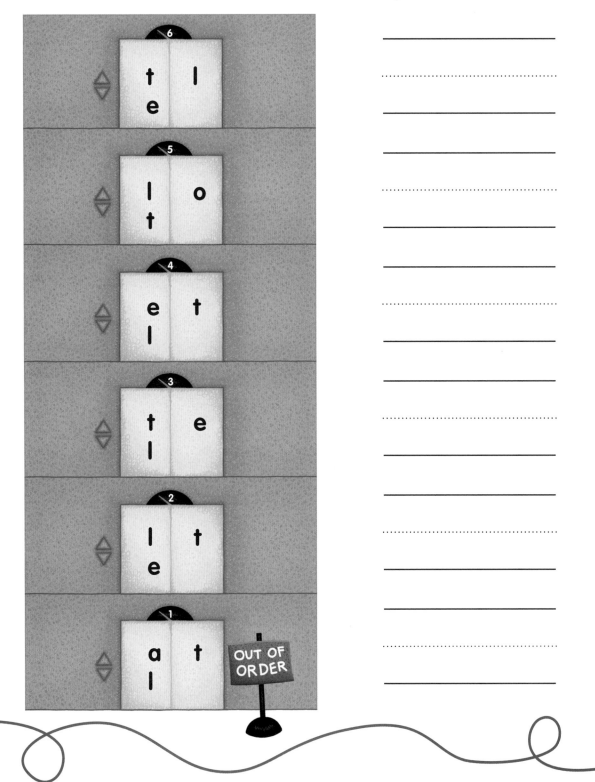

will say the word **will** aloud as you trace it.

will

Now practice writing the word once on each line.

We _____ have lunch soon.

58

Three Cheers

Circle the word **will** every time it appears. Count the number of circled words in each cheer and write it in the box.

Who will clap their hands?
Who will give a cheer?
Who will shout "Go Team"?
So everyone will hear!

Our team will play
Our team will score
And when they win
The crowd will roar

Team A

Team B

Which team's cheer has the higher number? _____

say the word **any** aloud as you trace it.

_____

Now practice writing the word once on each line.

Do you have _____ gum?

Hide and Seek

Some of the words in the treetop have **any** hidden inside. Find the words and write them on the lines below. Circle the letters **a-n-y** in each word.

animal   anyway   nanny   anyone
annoy   wonderful   answer
anybody   many   anywhere
anything

any

_____

_____

_____

_____

_____

_____

Review: Word Search!

Find each word in the word search.

him	please	let	will	any

```
t   w   h   p   w
h   i   m   l   i
l   l   l   e   t
p   l   y   a   s
a   n   w   s   n
a   p   e   e   h
```

Color the row that has all five review words spelled correctly.

1.	2.	3.	4.	5.
lef	him	will	let	please
will	please	amy	him	will
please	let	please	wiil	anv
hin	will	let	any	hlm
any	any	hin	please	let

Review: Black Out!

Read each sentence, then find the missing word in the boxes. Put an X through all the boxes that show the missing word.

A.

let	please
will	him

B.

any	him
will	let

1. Could you _____ open the door?

2. The dog needs to be _____ out.

3. You should take _____ outside.

4. _____ you take him on a walk?

5. Don't let him bark at _____ kids.

Which square has all its boxes marked off first? _____

went Say the word *went* **aloud as you trace it.**

went

Now practice writing the word once on each line.

I _____ down the slide.

Crack the Code

The word **went** is hidden once in each line. Find the word and circle the letters. Then use the code to complete the riddle below.

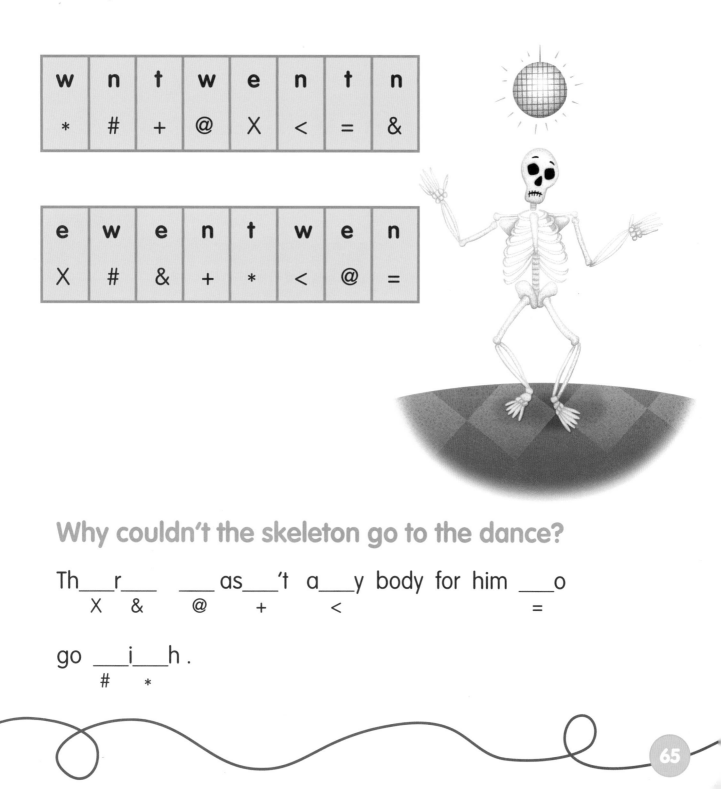

w	n	t	w	e	n	t	n
*	#	+	@	X	<	=	&

e	w	e	n	t	w	e	n
X	#	&	+	*	<	@	=

Why couldn't the skeleton go to the dance?

Th___r___ ___ as___'t a___y body for him ___o
   X   &   @   +   <   =

go ___i___h .
   #   *

new Say the word **new** aloud as you trace it.

new

Now practice writing the word once on each line.

I got a _____ bike.

Tic-Tac-Toe

Circle the row that spells the word **new**.

n	w	n
w	n	e
e	e	w

Circle the row that has the word **new** three times.

new	mew	new
mew	new	new
new	new	now

could

Say the word could aloud as you trace it.

could

Now practice writing the word once on each line.

I _____ eat the whole pie!

The Finish Line

Draw a line to link the letters that make the word could.

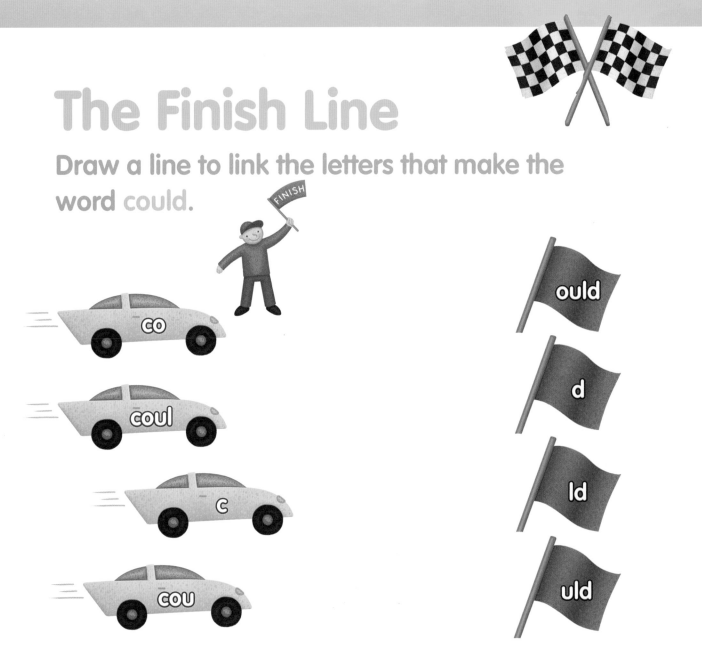

Do the letters in the flags make the word could? Circle Yes or No.

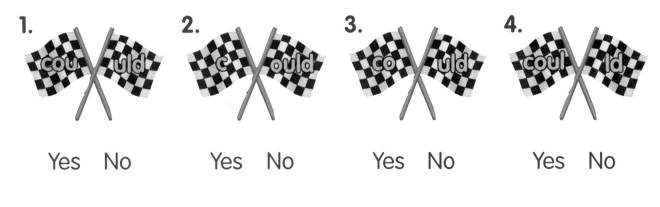

1. cou uld

Yes   No

2. c ould

Yes   No

3. co uld

Yes   No

4. coul ld

Yes   No

there say the word there aloud as you trace it.

there

Now practice writing the word once on each line.

My shoes are over _____.

Word Hunt

The word **there** is in the story five times. Hunt for the word and circle it each time it appears.

Where did all the cookies go? This morning there were three cookies. They were right there in the jar. Now there aren't any cookies! They're all gone! But I can still smell cookies. It's coming from over there by the oven. There is a new batch of cookies! I can't wait to eat them all up.

Circle the cookie jars with the word **there** inside.

1. there
2. there
3. their
4. thair
5. theer
6. there

 **eat**

Say the word eat aloud as you trace it.

 eat

Now practice writing the word once on each line.

It's time to _____.

Rhyme Time

Circle the pictures that rhyme with **eat**. Underline the letters **e-a-t** in each word.

heat

neat

ear

skate

tea

seat

meat

read

Review: Word Search

Find each word in the word search.

went   new   could   there   eat

```
t  e  a  t  c  o
h  a  w  e  n  c
t  h  e  r  e  o
e  n  a  l  n  u
w  e  w  d  e  l
e  w  e  n  t  d
```

Color the row that has all five review words spelled correctly.

1.	2.	3.	4.	5.
went	new	could	there	eat
nev	could	there	eat	went
could	theer	new	went	go
eet	went	weht	new	there
there	mew	eat	could	cuold

Review: Story Code

Look for the review words as you read the story.
Follow the code each time you see a review word.

went circle it

could make a box

eat put a check

new underline

there wavy line

Zack could not think of anything fun to do. He wanted to try something new. He decided to bake a pie that he could eat.

Then, his friend Josh came over with a new ball. The boys went outside to play with it. Zack forgot there was a pie baking in the oven.

"I'm so hungry, I could eat a pie," Josh said.

"There is a pie in the oven!" Zack said. The boys went inside. The pie was burned. There was nothing they could do.

"Let's bake a new pie," Josh said.

"And this time, let's make sure we get to eat it!" Zack said.

Review: Riddle

Use the code to fill in the missing letters and answer the knock knock joke.

came: **i**	black: **t**	are: **i**	have: **l**
soon: **o**	so: **n**	ride: **s**	ate: **A**
him: **c**	please: **r**	let: **e**	will: **h**
new: **o**	there: **d**	eat: **a**	

Knock knock.

Who's there?

_____ _____ _____ _____ _____.
ate   so   came   black   eat

_____ _____ _____ _____ _____ who?
ate   so   came   black   eat

_____ _____ _____ _____ _____
ate   so   came   black   eat

_____ _____ _____ _____ to
please   are   there   let

_____ _____ _____ _____ _____ _____!
ride   him   will   soon   new   have

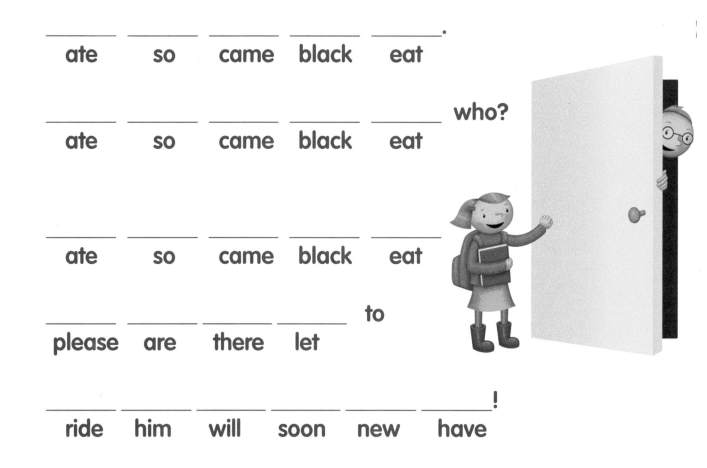

Review: Race

Look at each set of boxes. Find the word whose letters fit in the boxes.

going   at   under   do   must
brown   they   went   could   get
too   after   into   any   four

1. m u s t

2.

3.

4.

5.

6.

7.

8.

9.

10.

11.

12.

13.

14.

15.

now

Say the word **now** aloud as you trace it.

─────────

n o w

Now practice writing the word once on each line.

It's time for bed _____.

Stay on Track

Find the word **now** on each track and circle it.

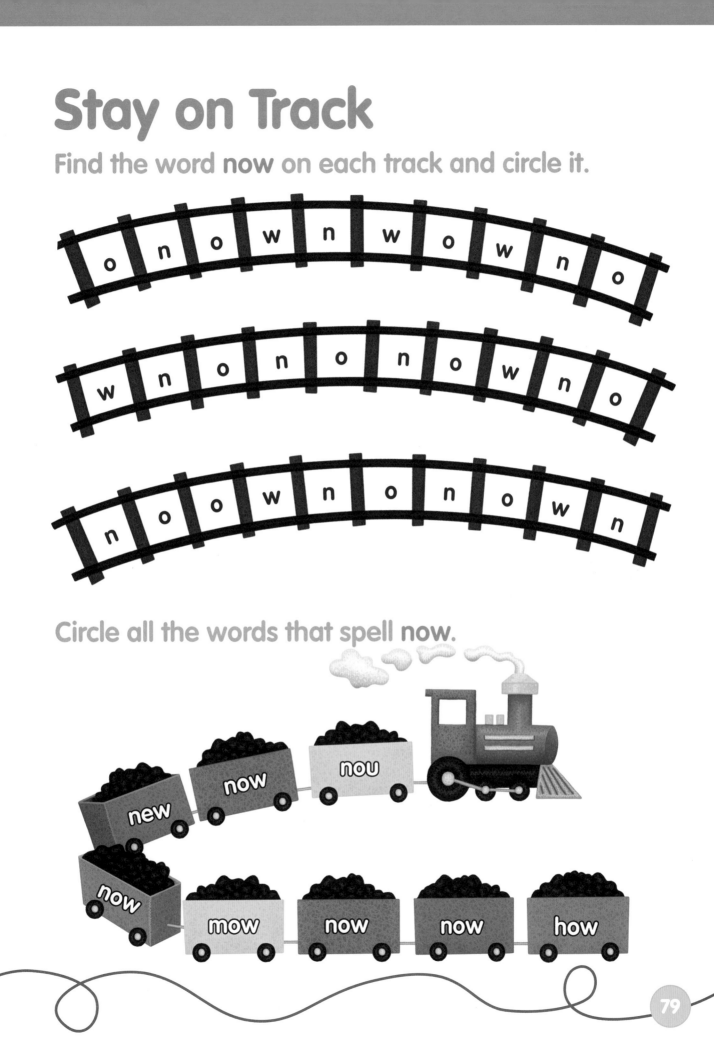

| o | n | o | w | n | w | o | w | n | o |

| w | n | o | n | o | n | o | w | n | o |

| n | o | o | w | n | o | n | o | w | n |

Circle all the words that spell **now**.

new

now

nou

now

mow

now

now

how

pretty *Say the word* **pretty** *aloud as you trace it.*

pretty

Now practice writing the word once on each line.

You look _____!

Maze Craze

Help the kitten find its way through the maze. Connect the letters **p-r-e-t-t-y** to make the word **pretty**.

 **this** **say the word this aloud as you trace it.**

Now practice writing the word once on each line.

I sit at _____ desk.

Out of Order

The letters for the word this are out of order! If the letters can be unscrambled to make the word this, write the word on the line. If not, leave it blank.

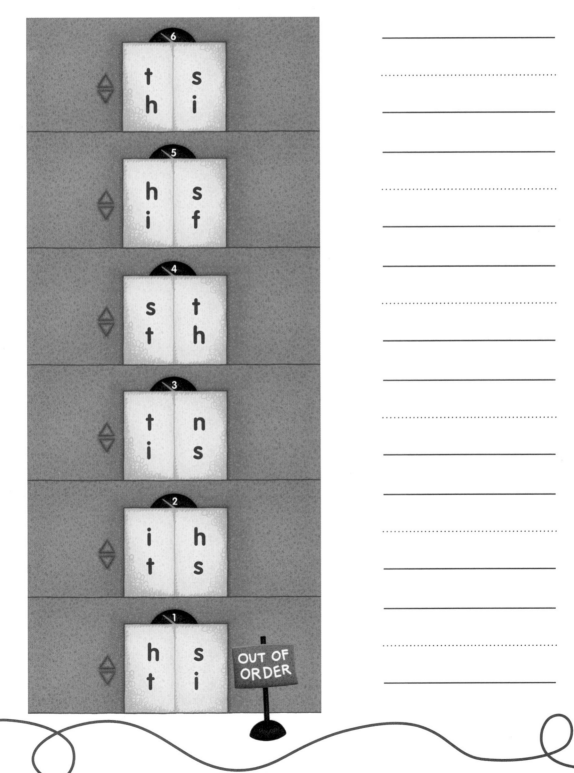

_____

....

_____

_____

....

_____

_____

....

_____

_____

....

_____

_____

....

_____

give say the word **give** aloud as you trace it.

----

give

Now practice writing the word once on each line.

I like to _____ my mom flowers.

Three Cheers

Circle the word **give** every time it appears. Count the number of circled words in each cheer and write it in the box.

Give me a W!
Give me an I!
Give me an N!
What does it spell?
Win!

Put your hands together. Give our team a shout! You can also give a cheer. That's what it's all about!

Team A

Team B

Which team's cheer has the higher number? _____

every Say the word **every** aloud as you trace it.

Now practice writing the word once on each line.

I do my homework _____ day.

Hide and Seek

Some of the words in the treetop have **every** hidden inside. Find the words and write them on the lines below. Circle the letters **e-v-e-r-y** in each word.

seven   clever   everybody

everyone

reverse

everywhere

evergreen

never

everything

event

every

_____

_____

_____

_____

Review: Word Search

Find each word in the word search.

| now | pretty | this | give | every |

```
e  p  g  i  v  e
v  r  i  n  o  r
y  e  v  e  r  y
n  t  i  i  v  t
o  t  h  s  g  t
w  y  t  h  i  s
```

Color the row that has all five review words spelled correctly.

1.	2.	3.	4.	5.
evrey	this	prety	now	nuw
this	giv	evry	pretty	this
now	every	give	give	prety
pritty	pretty	this	this	every
give	now	mow	every	giv

Review: Black Out!

Read each sentence, then find the missing word in the boxes. Put an X through all the boxes that show the missing word.

A.

give	pretty
this	every

B.

now	give
every	pretty

1. What can I _____ my mom for Mother's Day?

2. It seems like _____ year I buy flowers.

3. I want to get something new _____ year.

4. A _____ dress would be a nice gift.

5. All I need to do _____ is go buy one!

Which square has all its boxes marked off first? _____

 **say the word she aloud as you trace it.**

Now practice writing the word once on each line.

_____ is my sister.

Crack the Code

The word **she** is hidden once in each line. Find the word and circle the letters. Then use the code to complete the riddle below.

h	s	h	e	s	h	s	e
*	#	+	@	X	<	=	&

s	h	h	s	h	e	e	h
X	#	&	=	*	<	@	+

Why did the boy put sugar under his pillow?

So ___e would ___ave ___w___ ___t dream___.
   *   +   = < @   #

saw

Say the word saw aloud as you trace it.

_____

....
saw
_____

Now practice writing the word once on each line.

_____
....
_____
_____
....
_____
_____
_____
....
_____

I _____ a deer.

Tic-Tac-Toe

Circle the row that spells the word **saw**.

s	w	w
w	a	w
s	w	s

Circle the row that has the word **saw** three times.

saw	saw	swa
suw	saw	saw
sow	sew	saw

again say the word **again** aloud as you trace it.

Now practice writing the word once on each line.

I want to ride _____!

The Finish Line

Draw a line to the flag with the letters that finish the word **again**.

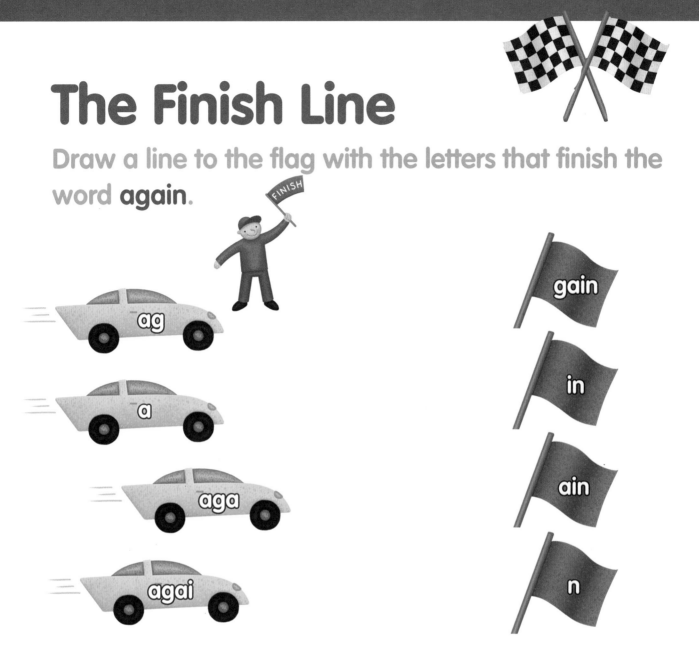

Do the letters in the flags make the word **again**?
Circle Yes or No.

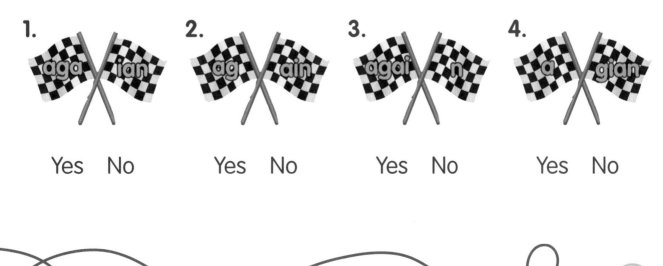

1. Yes   No   2. Yes   No   3. Yes   No   4. Yes   No

of

Say the word of aloud as you trace it.

of

Now practice writing the word once on each line.

My hat is on top _____ the books.

Word Hunt

The word **of** is in the story five times. Hunt for the word and circle it each time it appears.

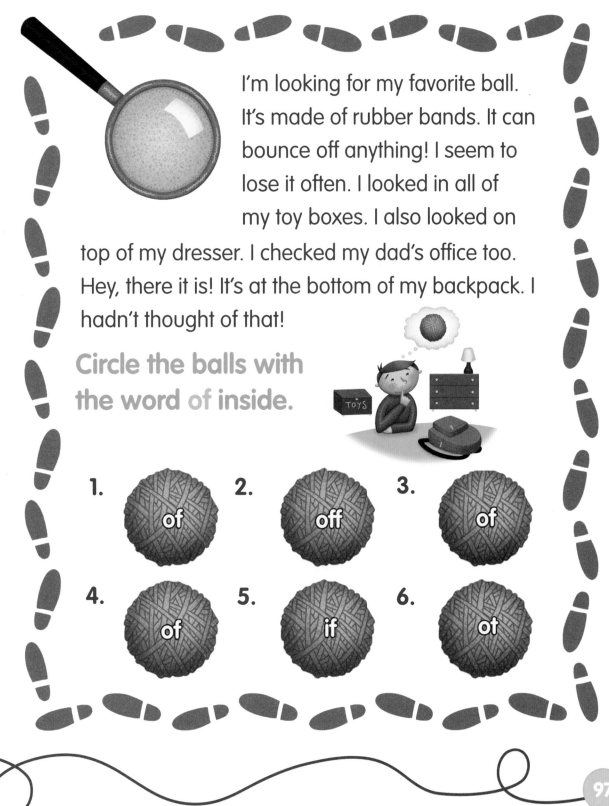

I'm looking for my favorite ball. It's made of rubber bands. It can bounce off anything! I seem to lose it often. I looked in all of my toy boxes. I also looked on top of my dresser. I checked my dad's office too. Hey, there it is! It's at the bottom of my backpack. I hadn't thought of that!

Circle the balls with the word of inside.

1. of
2. off
3. of
4. of
5. if
6. ot

our

Say the word **our** aloud as you trace it.

_____

our

Now practice writing the word once on each line.

This is _____ room.

Rhyme Time

Circle the pictures that rhyme with **our**. Underline the letters **o-u-r** in each word.

core

sour

turn

hour

scour

roar

floor

flour

Review: Word Search

Find each word in the word search.

| she | saw | again | of | our |

```
w  o  e  r  o
h  h  w  e  u
s  a  w  r  r
a  g  a  i  n
f  n  o  f  s
```

Color the row that has all five review words spelled correctly.

1.	2.	3.	4.	5.
again	of	uor	she	saw
swa	our	again	oru	she
she	again	she	saw	af
fo	she	ot	shi	again
our	saw	saw	of	our

Review: Story Code

Look for the review words as you read the story.
Follow the code each time you see a review word.

(she) circle it   <u>saw</u> underline

[again] make a box   of wavy line

✓our put a check

This morning we saw a kitten in our backyard. She was playing with a ball of yarn.

"None of our neighbors have a kitten," I said. "She must be lost."

When we looked up again, the kitten was gone.

Later that day, we saw her again. She was sleeping on top of our car.

"I saw a sign about a lost kitten at our bus stop," my dad said.

The sign had a picture of a kitten. It looked just like the kitten we saw!

We called the owners of the kitten. They came to pick her up at our house.

They were so happy to see their kitten again!

 **well** say the word **well** aloud as you trace it.

well

Now practice writing the word once on each line.

I can sing very _____.

Stay on Track

Find the word **well** on each track and circle it.

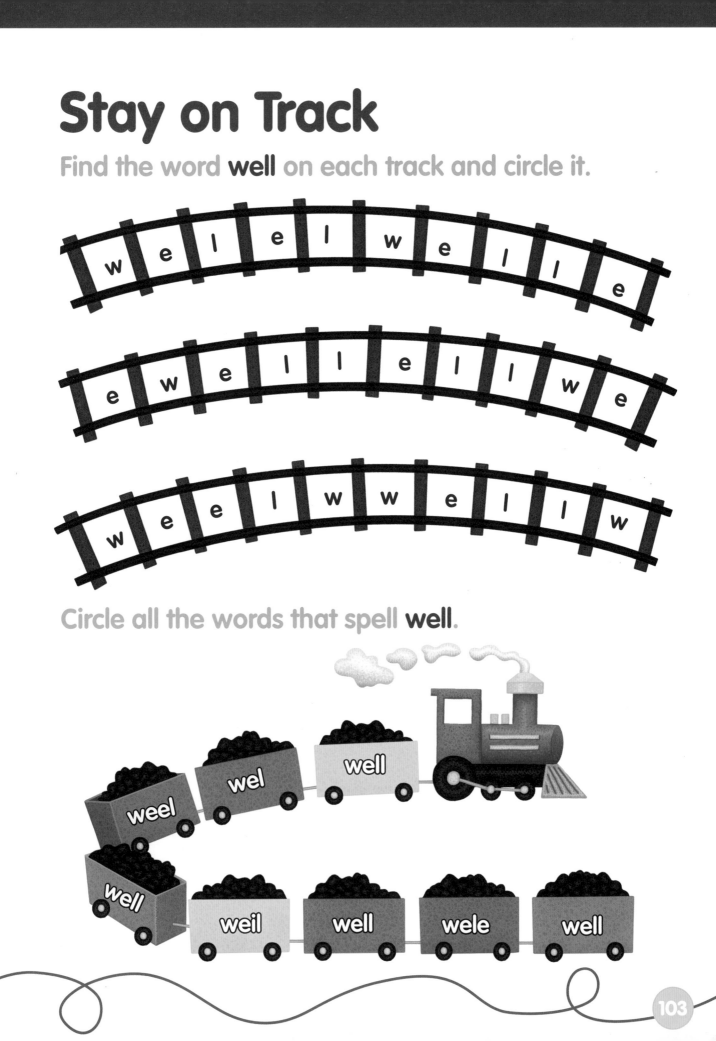

| w | e | l | e | l | w | e | l | l | e |

| e | w | e | l | l | e | l | l | w | e |

| w | e | e | l | w | w | e | l | l | w |

Circle all the words that spell **well**.

weel

wel

well

well

weil

well

wele

well

 **say the word white aloud as you trace it.**

Now practice writing the word once on each line.

The zebra is black and _____.

Maze Craze

Help the rabbit find its way through the maze. Connect the letters w-h-i-t-e to make the word white.

 **want**

Say the word
want aloud as
you trace it.

Now practice writing the word once on each line.

I _____ this book, please.

Out of Order

The letters for the word **want** are out of order! If the letters can be unscrambled to make the word **want**, write the word on the line. If not, leave it blank.

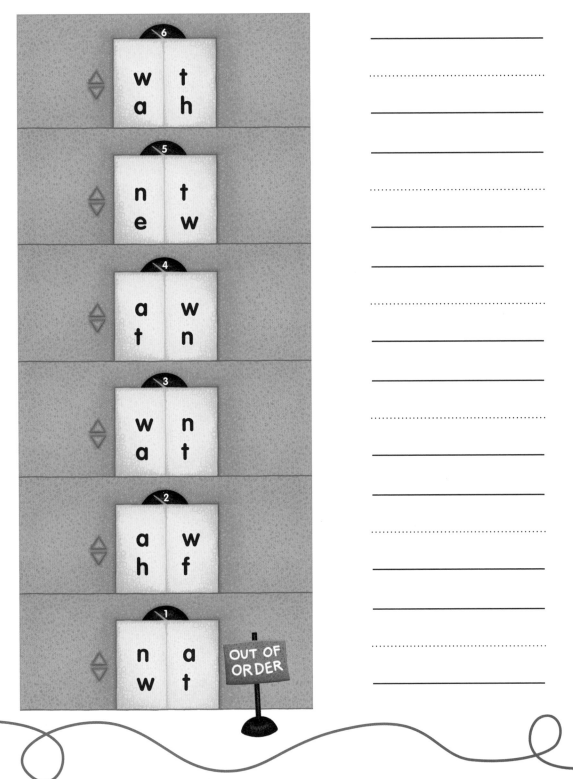

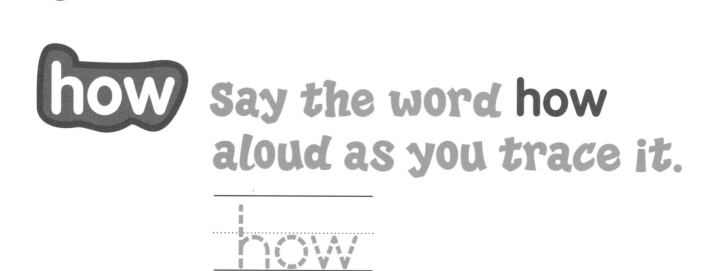

how say the word **how** aloud as you trace it.

how

Now practice writing the word once on each line.

_____ are you doing today?

Three Cheers

Circle the word **how** every time it appears. Count the number of circled words in each cheer and write it in the box.

We know how to play.
We know how to win.
We'll show them how it's done.
Now let's begin!

How will we beat the other team? How will we win tonight? We know how, and starting now, we'll show them how to do it right!

Team A

Team B

Which team's cheer has the higher number? _____

 **say the word some aloud as you trace it.**

_____

.... some ....

Now practice writing the word once on each line.

I have _____ of the apples.

Hide and Seek

Some of the words in the treetop have some hidden inside. Find the words and write them on the lines below. Circle the letters s-o-m-e in each word.

summer   sameness   smooth   somebody

something   handsome

someone   sometimes

somewhere   summary

some

_____

_____

_____

_____

_____

_____

Review: Word Search

Find each word in the word search.

| well | white | want | some | how |

```
h  o  s  m  w
w  a  n  t  e
s  o  m  e  l
o  h  o  w  l
w  h  i  t  e
```

Color the row that has all five review words spelled correctly.

1.	2.	3.	4.	5.
how	well	want	some	whate
want	white	some	whife	some
some	want	white	how	well
weil	some	huw	will	how
white	how	well	whant	want

Review: Black Out!

Read each sentence, then find the missing word in the boxes. Put an X through all the boxes that show the missing word.

A.

want	white
well	How

B.

some	How
want	well

1. Today my dad isn't feeling very _____.

2. He looks pale and _____.

3. _____ can I help him feel better?

4. I _____ to cheer him up.

5. I can make him _____ hot soup.

Which square has all its boxes marked off first? _____

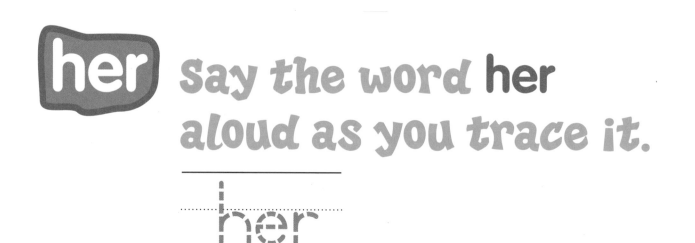

her say the word **her** aloud as you trace it.

her

Now practice writing the word once on each line.

I threw the ball to _____.

Crack the Code

The word **her** is hidden once in each line. Find the word and circle the letters. Then use the code to complete the riddle below.

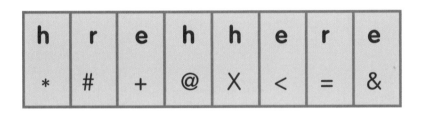

h	r	e	h	h	e	r	e
*	#	+	@	X	<	=	&

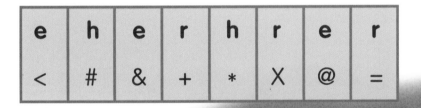

e	h	e	r	h	r	e	r
<	#	&	+	*	X	@	=

What do you do with a blue whale?

T___y to c___ ___ ___ ___ ___im up!

  =   # & < + X

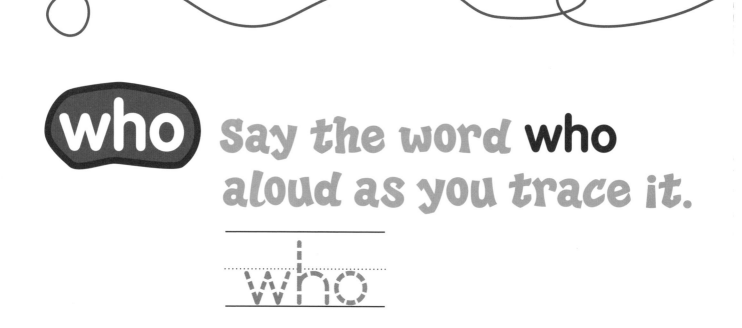

who say the word **who** aloud as you trace it.

who

Now practice writing the word once on each line.

_____ is it?

Tic-Tac-Toe

Circle the row that spells the word **who**.

w	w	h
w	h	w
o	w	o

Circle the row that has the word **who** three times.

wno	who	who
who	hoo	wha
who	who	who

round say the word round aloud as you trace it.

round

Now practice writing the word once on each line.

The table is _____.

The Finish Line

Draw a line to the flag with the letters that finish the word round.

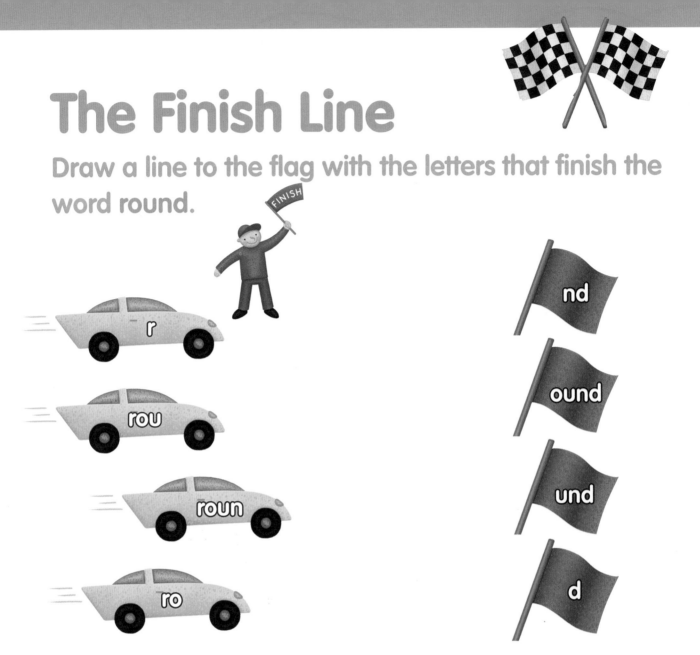

Do the letters in the flags make the word round?
Circle Yes or No.

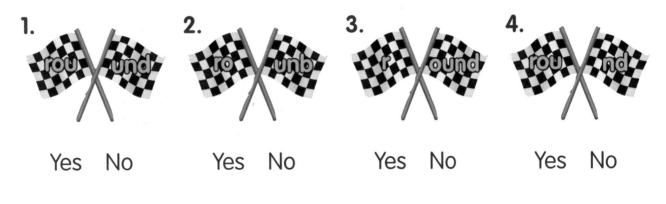

1. Yes   No

2. Yes   No

3. Yes   No

4. Yes   No

 **Say the word as aloud as you trace it.**

_____

as

Now practice writing the word once on each line.

I am as tall _____ my brother.

Word Hunt

The word **as** is in the story five times. Hunt for the word and circle it each time it appears.

Today I lost my hamster. She is very small. Her fur is white as snow. I looked all over the house, as did my mom. Just as I was about to give up, I heard a noise.

It sounded as if my hamster was in the bathtub. I looked in the tub, and there she was! She was playing with the bath toys, happy as can be.

Circle the ducks with the word **as** inside.

1. as
2. as
3. is
4. an
5. as
6. az

out Say the word **out** aloud as you trace it.

out

Now practice writing the word once on each line.

The dog ran _____ the door.

Rhyme Time

Circle the pictures that rhyme with **out**. Underline the letters **o-u-t** in each word.

shout

coat

spout

sprout

pout

note

flute

snout

Review: Word Search

Find each word in the word search.

her who round as out

```
r  o  u  r  d
w  s  e  o  n
w  h  e  u  a
r  n  o  n  s
o  u  t  d  h
```

Color the row that has all five review words spelled correctly.

1.	2.	3.	4.	5.
as	owt	her	round	who
who	her	rounb	out	as
out	round	as	vho	rounb
her	who	who	as	out
round	az	out	hir	hoo

Review: Story Code

Look for the review words as you read the story.
Follow the code each time you see a review word.

(her) circle it   who underline

[round] make a box   as wavy line

✓out put a check

On my sister's birthday, someone gave her a gift as a surprise. They left it out on our front steps. The box was big and round.

"Who is it from?" my sister asked.

"It doesn't say who it's from," I told her.

Just as we were about to open it, a puppy jumped out of the box! The puppy had big round eyes and fur white as snow. He licked her face and let out a bark. He was as cute as could be. We never found out who gave her the puppy. We loved it as one of the family.

from

Say the word **from** aloud as you trace it.

from

Now practice writing the word once on each line.

I got a letter _____ Grandma.

Stay on Track

Find the word **from** on each track and circle it.

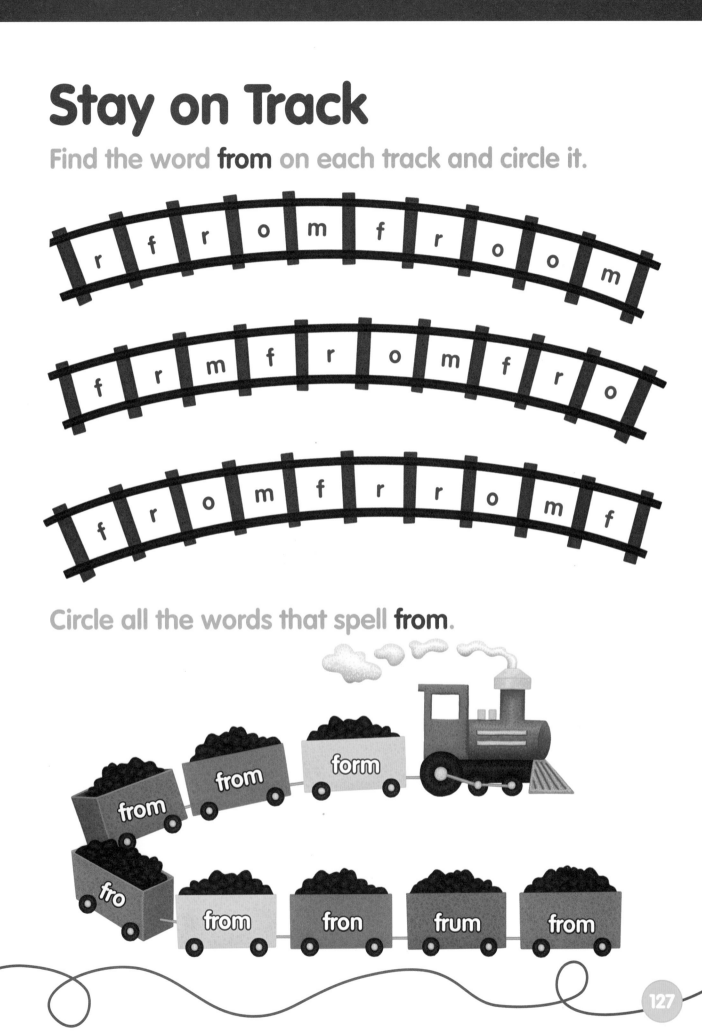

r f r o m f r o o m

f r m f r o m f r o

f r o m f r r o m f

Circle all the words that spell **from**.

from from form

fro from fron frum from

with *say the word* with *aloud as you trace it.*

with

Now practice writing the word once on each line.

I shared my lunch _____ him.

Out of Order

The letters for the word **with** are out of order! If the letters can be unscrambled to make the word with, write the word on the line. If not, leave it blank.

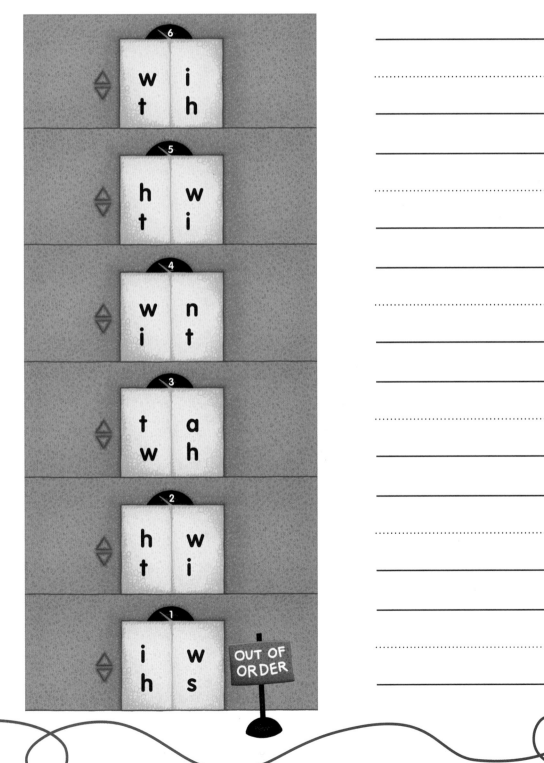

say the word had aloud as you trace it.

had

Now practice writing the word once on each line.

I _____ pizza for dinner.

Tic-Tac-Toe

Circle the row that spells the word **had**.

a	h	a
d	a	d
h	d	h

Circle the row that has the word **had** three times.

had	had	had
had	had	hand
dad	bad	hod

 **thank** say the word **thank** aloud as you trace it.

Now practice writing the word once on each line.

I want to _____ you for helping me.

The Finish Line

Draw a line to the flag with the letters that finish the word **thank**.

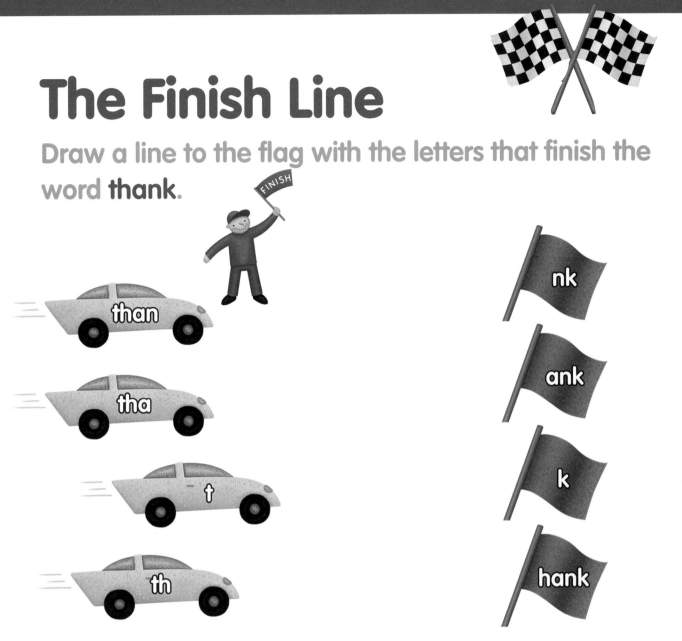

than

tha

t

th

nk

ank

k

hank

Do the letters in the flags make the word **thank**?
Circle Yes or No.

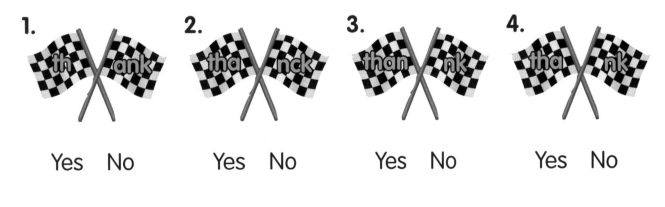

1. th ank

Yes   No

2. tha nck

Yes   No

3. than nk

Yes   No

4. tha nk

Yes   No

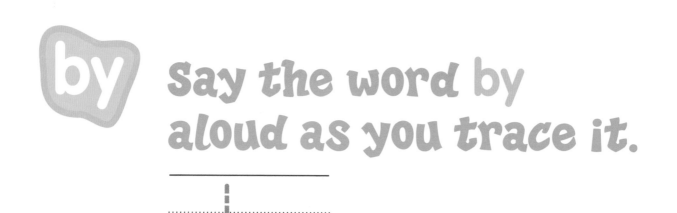

by **Say the word by aloud as you trace it.**

by

Now practice writing the word once on each line.

My bag is _____ the chair.

Word Hunt

The word **by** is in the story five times. Hunt for the word and circle it each time it appears.

I lost my book. It's written by my favorite author. I can read the whole book by myself. I like to read it before I go to bed. By the time I find it, it will be too late to read it. I have to go to bed by eight o'clock. Maybe tomorrow I can buy a new book. Wait! I found it! It was right by my bed all along.

Circle the books with the word by inside.

1. by

2. buy

3. busy

4. dy

5. by

6. by

Review: Word Search

Find each word in the word search.

a	from	with	had	thank	by

i	w	i	t	h
f	h	b	h	i
r	i	h	a	d
o	m	a	n	r
m	b	y	k	f

Color the row that has all five review words spelled correctly.

1.	2.	3.	4.	5.
bv	thank	with	had	from
thank	had	thanx	for	with
from	wifh	had	dy	had
with	by	fron	from	thank
hab	from	by	thank	by

Review: Black Out!

Read each sentence, then find the missing word in the boxes. Put an X through all the boxes that show the missing word.

A.

from	had
by	with

B.

with	thank
had	by

1. A new boy moved into the house _____ mine.

2. He moved here _____ Japan.

3. We asked him to have dinner _____ us.

4. We _____ a great dinner.

5. He gave us a gift to _____ us.

Which square has all its boxes marked off first? _____

Review: Riddle

Use the code to fill in the missing letters and answer the knock knock joke.

pretty: **t**	our: **i**	her: **i**	out: **e**
this: **n**	white: **c**	who: **s**	with: **u**
every: **t**	how: **n**	round: **m**	had: **h**
saw: **J**	some: **u**	as: **l**	

Knock knock.
Who's there?

____ ____ ____ ____ ____ ____.
saw   some who   every our   how

____ ____ ____ ____ ____ ____ **who?**
saw   some who   every our   how

____ ____ ____ ____ ____ ____
saw   some who   every our   how

____ ____ ____ ____
pretty her   round out

for ____ ____ ____ ____ ____ !
     as   with   this   white had

Review: Race

Look at each set of boxes. Find the word whose letters fit in the boxes.

of	she	want	from	again
by	now	give	well	thank

1. of

2.

3.

4.

5.

6.

7.

8.

9.

10.

Answer Key

Page 5

3rd floor: four
5th floor: four

Page 11
(Do) we want to win?
Yes, we (do)!
We'll (do) all we can.
How about you?
Team A: 3

We'll (do) just great!
We'll (do) our best.
How (do) we do it?
We'll (do) better than the rest!
Team B: 5

Team B has the higher number.

Page 7

Page 13
These words have **too** hidden inside:
tool
stoop
tooth
cartoon
stool
toot

Page 14

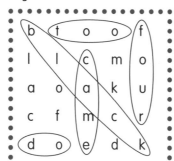

Row 3 is colored.

Page 15
1. too
2. came
3. black
4. do
5. four
Square B has all its boxes marked off first.

Page 17
Because it stays out all night long!

Page 19

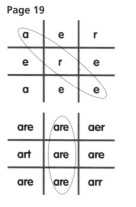

Page 21

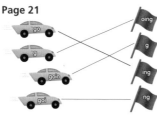

1. No
2. Yes
3. No
4. Yes

Page 23
(Have) you seen my hat? I (have) been looking for half the day. I need some help to find it. I usually hang it in the hall. I (have) a special hook for my hat. But it's not there! I (have) to find it soon. My head needs a hat. It's the only hat I (have).

These hats are circled:
1. have
3. have
4. have

Page 25
These pictures are circled:
hat
rat
bat
mat
cat

Page 26

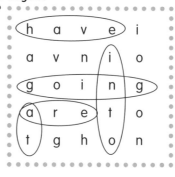

Row 3 is colored.

Page 27
I always have my birthday party at home. This year, I wanted to have it someplace new.
   "We are going somewhere different," my family said. "You are going to have a great time."
   We all got into the car.
   "Where are we going?" I asked.
   "It's a surprise," they said. "You have to close your eyes."
   "Are we there yet?" I asked.
   "You have to be patient!" they said.
   After a long drive, the car stopped.
   "We're at the beach!" I said.
   We all jumped into the water.

Page 29

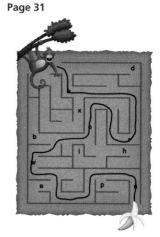

Page 31

(maze illustration)

Page 33
3rd floor: soon
4th floor: soon
6th floor: soon

Page 35
When I (say) "go" you (say) "fight." Go! Go! Fight! Fight! When I (say) "win" you (say) "tonight." Win! Win! Tonight! Tonight!
Team A: 4

You (say) you're so great. You (say) you're the best. But we're here to (say) we're better than the rest.
Team B: 3

Team A has the higher number.

Page 37

These words have **under** hidden inside:
<u>th</u><u>under</u>
<u>understand</u>
<u>underneath</u>
<u>underwear</u>
<u>underground</u>

Page 38

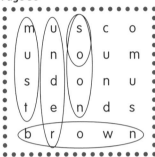

Row 4 is colored.

Page 39

1. so
2. soon
3. must
4. brown
5. under
Square B has all its boxes marked off first.

Page 41

She wan<u>ted</u> to save <u>it</u> for a <u>rainy</u> <u>day</u>.

Page 43

e	t	g
g	e	t
g	t	e

got	pet	get
get	get	gte
get	get	get

Page 45

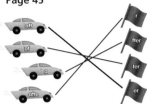

1. Yes
2. Yes
3. No
4. No

Page 47

I have twin brothers, Tim and Jim. They look exactly the same. They have brown hair and blue eyes. Today they have on matching clothes. Both of them are wearing white shirts and jeans. Hey, I can't tell them apart! I hope they tell me who is who. If not, then they will be in big trouble!

These shirts are circled:
2. they
3. they
4. they

Page 49

These words are circled:
<u>date</u>
<u>gate</u>
<u>late</u>
<u>plate</u>

Page 50

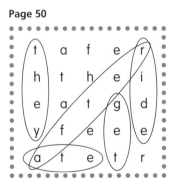

Row 5 is colored.

Page 51

Amy and Ella went to the fair. First they saw the animals. A pony a<u>te</u> a carrot out of Ella's hand. After that, Ella wanted to go on a ride.

"Let's ride the Ferris wheel," Ella said.

"We need to <u>get</u> some tickets first," Amy said.

After they got tickets, they went on the ride. Then they decided to <u>get</u> hot dogs.

After they a<u>te</u>, they went home. They decided to come to the fair every year!

Page 53

Page 55

Page 57

2nd floor: let
3rd floor: let
4th floor: let
6th floor: let

Page 59

Who will clap their hands?
Who will give a cheer?
Who will shout "Go Team"?
So everyone will hear!
Team A: 4

Our team will play
Our team will score
And when they win
The crowd will roar
Team B: 3

Team A has the higher number.

Page 61

These words have **any** hidden inside:
m<u>any</u>
<u>any</u>one
<u>any</u>where
<u>any</u>body
<u>any</u>way
<u>any</u>thing

Page 62

Row 2 is colored.

Page 63

1. please
2. let
3. him
4. Will
5. any
Square A has all its boxes marked off first.

Page 65

There <u>wasn't</u> <u>any</u>body for him <u>to</u> go <u>with</u>.

Page 67

n	w	n
w	n	e
e	e	w

new	mew	new
mew	new	new
new	new	now

Page 69

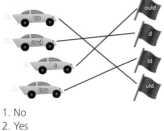

1. No
2. Yes
3. Yes
4. No

Page 71

Where did all the cookies go? This morning (there) were three cookies. They were right (there) in the jar. Now, (there) aren't any cookies! They're all gone! But I can still smell cookies. It's coming from over (there) by the oven. (There) is a new batch of cookies! I can't wait to eat them all up.

These cookie jars are circled:
1. there
2. there
6. there

Page 73

These words are circled:
heat
neat
seat
meat

Page 74

t	e	a	t	c	o
h	a	w	e	n	c
t	h	e	r	e	o
e	n	a	l	n	u
w	e	w	d	e	l
e	w	e	n	t	d

Row 4 is colored.

Page 75

Zack could not think of anything fun to do. He wanted to try something new. He decided to bake a pie that he could eat.

Then, his friend Josh came over with a new ball. The boys went outside to play with it. Zack forgot there was a pie baking in the oven.

"I'm so hungry, I could eat a pie," Josh said.

"There is a pie in the oven!" Zack said. The boys went inside. The pie was burned. There was nothing they could do.

"Let's bake a new pie," Josh said.

"And this time, let's make sure we get to eat it!" Zack said.

Page 76

Knock knock.
Who's there?
Anita.
Anita who?
Anita ride to school!

Page 77

2. do
3. any
4. get
5. too
6. four
7. into
8. at
9. they
10. went
11. could
12. going
13. brown
14. under
15. after

Page 79

Page 81

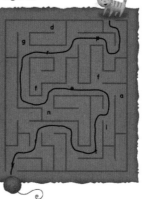

Page 83

1st floor: this
2nd floor: this
6th floor: this

Page 85

(Give) me a W!
(Give) me an I!
(Give) me an N!
What does it spell?
Win!
Team A: 3

Put your hands together.
(Give) your team a shout!
You can also (give) a cheer.
That's what it's all about!
Team B: 2

Team A has the higher number.

Page 87

These words have **every** hidden inside:
everybody
everywhere
everyone
everything

Page 88

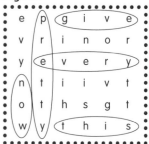

e	p	g	i	v	e
v	r	i	n	o	r
y	e	v	e	r	y
n	t	i	i	v	t
o	t	h	s	g	t
w	y	t	h	i	s

Row 4 is colored.

Page 89

1. give
2. every
3. this
4. pretty
5. now
Square A has all its boxes marked off first.

Page 91

So he would have sweet dreams.

Page 93

s	w	w
w	a	w
s	w	s

saw	saw	swa
saw	saw	saw
sow	sew	saw

Page 95

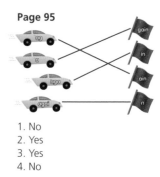

1. No
2. Yes
3. Yes
4. No

142

Page 97

I'm looking for my favorite ball. It's made of rubber bands. It can bounce off anything! I seem to lose it often. I looked in all of my toy boxes. I also looked on top of my dresser. It checked my dad's office too. Hey, there it is! It's at the bottom of my backpack. I hadn't thought of that!

These balls are circled:
1. of
3. of
4. of

Page 99

These words are circled:
sour
hour
scour
flour

Page 100

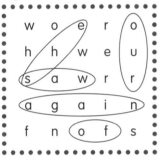

Row 2 is colored.

Page 101

This morning we saw a kitten in our backyard. She was playing with a ball of yarn.
"None of our neighbors have a kitten," I said. "She must be lost."
When we looked up again, the kitten was gone.
Later that day, we saw her again. She was sleeping on top of our car.
"I saw a sign about a lost kitten at our bus stop," my dad said.
The sign had a picture of a kitten. It looked just like the kitten we saw!
We called the owners of the kitten. They came to pick her up at our house.
They were so happy to see their kitten again!

Page 103

Page 105

Page 107

3rd floor: want
4th floor: want
6th floor: want

Page 109

We know how to play.
We know how to win.
We'll show them how it's done.
Now let's begin!
Team A: 3

How will we beat the other team?
How will we win tonight?
We know how and starting now, we'll show them how to do it right!
Team B: 4

Team B has the higher number.

Page 111

These words have **some** hidden inside:
somewhere
somebody
someone
sometimes
handsome
something

Page 112

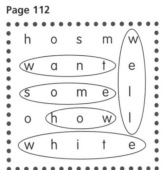

Row 2 is colored.

Page 113

1. well
2. white
3. How
4. want
5. some

Square A has all its boxes marked off first.

Page 115

Try to cheer him up!

Page 117

w	w	h
w	h	w
o	w	o

wno	who	who
who	hoo	wha
who	who	who

Page 119

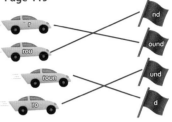

1. No
2. No
3. Yes
4. Yes

Page 121

Today I lost my hamster. She is very small. Her fur is white as snow. I looked all over the house, as did my mom. Just as I was about to give up, I heard a noise. It sounded as if my hamster was in the bathtub. I looked in the tub, and there she was! She was playing with the bath toys, happy as she could be.

These ducks are circled:
1. as
2. as
5. as

Page 123

These words are circled:
shout
pout
sprout
snout
spout

Page 124

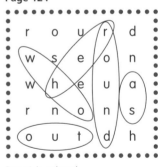

Row 1 is colored.

Page 125

On my sister's birthday, someone gave her a gift as a surprise. They left it out on our front steps. The box was big and round.

"Who is it from?" my sister asked.

"It doesn't say who it's from," I told her.

Just as we were about to open it, a puppy jumped out of the box! The puppy had big round eyes and fur white as snow. He licked her face and let out a bark. He was as cute as could be. We never found out who gave her the puppy. We loved it as one of the family.

Page 127

Page 129

2nd floor: with
5th floor: with
6th floor: with

Page 131

a	h	a
d	a	d
h	d	h

had	had	had
had	had	hand
dad	bad	hod

Page 133

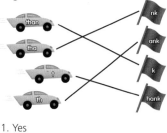

1. Yes
2. No
3. No
4. Yes

Page 135

I lost my book. It's written by my favorite author. I can read the whole book by myself. I like to read it before I go to bed. By the time I find it, it will be too late to read it. I have to go to bed by eight o'clock. Maybe tomorrow I can buy a new book. Wait! I found it! It was right by my bed all along.

These books are circled:
1. by
5. by
6. by

Page 136

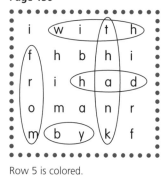

Row 5 is colored.

Page 137

1. by
2. from
3. with
4. had
5. thank

Square A has all its boxes marked off first.

Page 138

Knock, knock.
Who's there?
Justin.
Justin who?
Justin time for lunch!

Page 139

2. she
3. by
4. want
5. now
6. give
7. well
8. from
9. thank
10. again